food for thoughtful parenting

12 must-have lists for new parents & young families

nina coslov & tara keppler

ISBN-978-0-578-04332-6

Book design by Tara Keppler
Printed in Canada.
Published by Six Monkey Press, Cambridge, MA

for
Liv, Bump, and Per
&
Zan, Will, and Kate

contents

introduction

Our goal for this book was to create a collection of lists that pulled together some of our favorite parenting strategies and tactics. We've gathered these ideas over years on playground benches, during parking lot chats, and through our own trial-and-error experiences. They are the ideas that best help us ease the way through rough spots, inject new energy into the time we spend with our families, and remind us to be the parents we want to be more of the time: relaxed, proactive, creative, supportive, and present. We share these with the hope that they might do the same for you.

Nina & Tara

food for thoughtful parenting...

Thoughts for Newbies

1. Find your people
2. Let go
3. Find your own way
4. Embrace a new rhythm
5. Back off

1. Find your people. What do we mean by "your people?" It's changed. Your people are no longer your childhood friends, your college friends, your favorites from that book group. Your people are now anyone who became a new parent within two to three weeks of you. Where to find them? A few suggestions: join a local new parent's group. Many hospitals and birth centers facilitate these groups. Start up a conversation if you see someone with an infant while you are at the pediatrician's office, out for a walk, or at the grocery store. Make a point to notice new parents at the library, park, or gym. Check out how they interact with their babies and what kind of gear they're toting around—you'll likely be able to identify people with whom you'll have something in common. When you find your people, you'll know. They are struggling with, enjoying, and being blown away by the same things as you on exactly the same time schedule. And it is likely they are facing the same repercussions of sleep deprivation. When it's a good match, these will be some of your most treasured and enduring relationships—period. They're friendships that will greatly ease and enrich your journey to new parenthood.

For me there's nothing that could ever rival the sense of comfort, support, and hope I got from my new-found "mama friends" during that crazy transitional time when we'd commiserate about cracked nipples, in-laws, body image, the color of poop, sex. No way I would have been so hopeful, playful, or confident, or laughed so much that first year without them! —t

2. Let go. The demands and delight of a new baby leave much less time in your day to get the other stuff done. Here are two of our favorite ways to deal with this challenge: first, let go of some things to make room for what matters more. As new parents, we both heard tips such as "don't clean the house," "let the laundry pile up," "sleep when the baby sleeps," or "don't return phone calls." For one of us a messy house is cause for distress and anxiety ... for the other it is not getting to the phone at least daily to connect with friends. Take the time to figure out what things bring you peace and enjoyment in these changing times and which tasks you can really "let go."

Second, allow yourself to accept help—which can be harder than it seems. For us, one of the toughest things to "let go" of was our sense of independence and competence. We had cruised along for so many years smugly in control in the driver's seat, takin' care of business just fine, thank you. Amazingly, a thoughtful offer of assistance somehow cast a shadow of self-doubt, and we thought, "Am I someone who needs help?!" Pause. Reframe it. Ask yourself, instead, "Why wouldn't I accept this kind gesture in order to have more time to bond with my baby, spend with my family, relax, sleep, work out, get to the phone (fill in the things that bring you peace and enjoyment here!) … ?" So our advice? Say yes, thank you, and let the help in! Savor the meal, soak in the clean tub, be grateful that the onesies are clean—even if they are folded in a funny shape.

3. Find your own way. Your parenting legs will stabilize daily. This stabilization goes on and on throughout your parenting journey. Seek advice from those you trust. Good friends and books can confirm your instincts when you feel wobbly about your choices. There is a book out there that supports every parenting style. Find yours. But no matter what you read or hear, trust your gut. Figure out what works for you and your family, and have confidence in your own deep connection and understanding of your child, whether it's breast or bottle, disposable or cloth, sling or stroller, full time or part time, bunny or bear, or any combination. And as your child grows, reassess what approaches still work and which to revise.

As a new parent, it helps to be prepared for the inevitable barrage of advice that will come your way. Although advice is usually well-intentioned and often useful, a lot of advice is unsolicited, and some is downright intrusive. We found it handy to have a couple of responses ready for those conversations we'd rather avoid: "Thanks, you've really given me something to think about," or "It's good to get other perspectives," or "Wow, I wouldn't have thought of that." And for the truly unhelpful pieces of advice: "Thanks, I'll suggest that to her parents."

4. Embrace a new rhythm. Read "rhythm," not "schedule," here. Yes, the schedule (if you choose to create one) of your day will change, too, but by rhythm we mean the flow of your day. Those four-hour chunks of time you previously had to indulge on a task are now shorter—much. Babies need to be fed, put to sleep, and changed with astonishing frequency. So those four-hour chunks are now plus or minus 30 minutes. It may be shocking and overwhelming at first—it was for us. No matter how long (or short) those bits of time are in the beginning, they do get longer and longer. Hey, by the time your child is two, you may even have 45 minutes to yourself!

- -

I remember this sense of dread every time my newborn cried and my mom would say, "I think he's hungry." I thought, "Already? He can't be!" It felt suffocating. The sooner I recognized, rather than fought, the need to give into a new rhythm, the easier things felt. —n

- -

5. Back off. By this we mean let your child have their own relationships with other people without your (over) involvement. This can be hard, particularly with relatives—we all have ways that we want our children to be treated, to be spoken to, and in turn (when they're older) to treat others and to speak to them. It's easy to get hung up on trying to be an arbitrator between, say, a child and a grandparent. Once your friends or relatives understand your family rules (such as no coffee drinks or video games for toddlers), you should get out of the way. It is important, and beneficial, for children to experience different personalities and realize that there are inconsistencies in the world. Even if a grandparent buys them ice cream for lunch, it doesn't mean that you will. And when your own family values are clear to your kids, have faith that your children will understand that even though it's fun, it is a little nutty for Granny to come over with donuts at 9 p.m.!

- -

I woke up one morning to find that my husband had made breakfast for our daughter. Then I saw it. Eggs. And a banana! "She doesn't eat those anymore," I quietly warned. "Daddy and I are having breakfast!" Liv declared with delight, happily eating both eggs and banana. She wouldn't eat a banana from me, but from Daddy, she would. Our kids' relationships with other people are dynamic, and they are not the same as their relationships with us. She is my daughter, but she's also that girl's friend, that man's grandchild, and my husband's daughter, too. —t

- -

Gifts to Yourself

1. Care for your friendships
2. Share a passion
3. Give yourself a head start
4. Learn something new
5. Get out!

1. Care for your friendships. Old friendships are stabilizing forces in our lives and often the thing that quickly gets pushed aside as partners, jobs, and growing families take center stage. For those who have moved around a lot it can be particularly hard to stay in touch. Our advice: reframe getting in touch with a friend as a gift to yourself rather than an item on your to-do list. You'll be more likely to make the call or send the email. Keep up contact with those people who know you in other contexts. When you feel yourself lost in the—yes, sometimes thankless—role of parent, what a gift to have the other parts of yourself drawn to the surface: the colleague, the one in the glamorous dress, the athlete, the karaoke star.

- -

I made the mistake of thinking that my oldest and dearest friend from high school—who didn't yet have kids— would be bored by the minutiae of my daily grind with a newborn, and I found myself feeling a strange reluctance to call. Certainly a conversation about diapering, *nursing, and the challenge of getting the laundry done would be of little interest when we were used to talking about music, things we were reading, and boys. Another friend set me straight, pointing out that while she might not have the same level of concern with the details of my baby-driven day, it was **me** she cared about, whatever it was I was going through. —t*

- -

2. Share a passion. Reconnect with your own pre-kid passion for something (pottery, biking, electric guitar, baking, sewing, fishing). Think about how to explain, explore and share this with your child. Doing such an activity together can be an inspiration to your child and lets her know about an important part of who you are separate from your role as her parent. Don't worry if she doesn't show particular interest in the subject. The point is that she senses engagement and passion in you: that alone makes an important statement.

- -

As someone who loves the outdoors, it was a real gift to me to see my children connecting to things outside. Signs of fall, the first buds of spring, the first snowfall, bugs, and even the most common birds—all were experienced anew through their eyes. —t

- -

3. Give yourself a head start. If your dream day starts at 11:45 a.m. with coffee in bed, this isn't for you. But if you find yourself feeling behind all day, try getting up a little earlier. Starting your day quietly and on your own terms can help set the right tone for the hours that follow. Get up before the rest of the household starts to stir. Do whatever it is that allows you to feel ready for the day. Read the paper, exercise, check e-mail, scratch something off your list, eat breakfast slowly. Even rising 30 minutes before a toddler is asking for food can start your day off on a good footing.

4. Learn something new. Whether it's taking a class in something that caught your eye or picking up a new "how to" manual at the library, think about cultivating a new talent or interest. Committing to a class has the added bonus of forcing you to get out of the house and creates an opportunity to interact with the adult world around a common interest. Once you've paid and put something on your calendar, you'll be more likely to follow through with that knitting project, the spinning class at the gym, or a new adventure in photography. You may feel pressed for time, but an hour here and there spent on yourself does wonders for the other (many!) hours you spend for all the other people who demand your time.

5. Get out! With your child or alone—get outside. Being stuck inside or tied to a young child's schedule can feel very isolating. While deliberate social gigs help,

don't forget about simply connecting with what's around you. You don't need a national park, a big city itinerary, or even a destination. Around the block can sometimes be just the ticket, and a walk in the woods or along the river is a lovely way to spend 30 minutes, an hour or two. It is easy with young children to just stay put: all the extra stuff you need to do and take along can quash the best of intentions. Making the effort is time well spent, guaranteed. Take your kid along in a stroller or pack, and get out!

My son was born in late November in Boston, and at first I really struggled to get out of the house. He needed so many layers, I needed so many layers—then there were the extra diapers, wipes, changing pad, change of clothes, pacifier, burp cloth, and little toy for distraction that I thought I had to pack into my big diaper bag. Most of the time I just didn't go, and when I did, I was sweating and exhausted before we even got out the door. What I learned: all I needed was the baby in fleece and a carrier strapped to my front, and we were good to go. The fresh air and change of scenery did wonders for my state of mind in those early days. —n

Teaching and Learning

1. Share the thinking
2. Let discovery happen
3. Break it down
4. See the good
5. Tell a story

1. Share the thinking. As parents we all feel the pressure of setting a good example for our children by modeling good behavior. We try to be kind, helpful, considerate, and polite. What we offer here is the idea of taking this a step further when your own situation presents a good learning opportunity for your kids. For example, when you make a mistake, don't know an answer, or hurt someone's feelings, let your children in on the process of acknowledging the mistake, finding the answer, or apologizing. "Oh man, I messed up—I did the wrong thing!" can be the start of a rich conversation about disappointment, taking responsibility, or affecting an outcome. Tell them how you're "taking a few quiet minutes" to settle down when things get heated or frustrating. Explain how making that phone call wasn't a good choice, since it made you late. Or share a realization and how you plan to fix it: "I made a mistake and I think I hurt her feelings. I need to talk to her so I can apologize." Really say all that stuff out loud. Break down the pieces and talk about the things that add to the situation. Share and name your feelings—when you're

frustrated or disappointed, jealous or sad, proud or relieved. You'll help your child understand the situation, and help them develop their emotional vocabulary as they learn to label their own experiences. And the more articulate children can be about their feelings, the easier it will be to support them.

2. Let discovery happen. It can be hard to resist the urge to make every moment a "teaching moment." But when kids are allowed to explore unguided and just left to experiment on their own, they will take ownership of their discovery and their learning will crystallize on a deeper level. As parents, we can undermine our child's learning and enjoyment of an experience by inserting our eagerness to interpret. Yes, there are useful tips to pass along (try to catch a ball somewhere other than in front of your face, it's easier to hold the scissors like this), and basic guiding rules (keep the paint on the paper, don't eat the clay). And for sure, you are your child's teacher. But beyond what's necessary for safety's sake, try to allow learning to happen for them on their own. Parental upside? The glimmer in their eyes when they've learned something new of their own accord.

3. Break it down. Many things we ask of our kids are complicated: "Time to go! Get ready!" or "This room is a mess. Please clean it up." These comments and commands represent large tasks with many steps that we as adults intuitively know how to approach. But for young kids these requests may be overwhelming. Imagine that

you join an assembly line and are asked to "put together the dashboard." Eventually, with someone systematically breaking down and explaining each step, you'd probably be able to complete the task. For kids, it's the same: when the task is complex, break it down into manageable bits, with specific directions and doable pieces. To "get ready to go," a child has to stop playing; put away the toy; find shoes. For "clean up," requests such as "First put the blocks in the crate" followed by "Please put those books on the shelf" are really critical to allowing a child to be successful at helping.

When I question this need to unpack all the details, I remember one of my favorite "break-it-downs" from when my son was potty training and learning to wipe himself. I showed him how much toilet paper to use, and how to fold it. I don't know if I expected embarrassment or laughter when I said, "You have to look on the toilet paper to see if there's any poo on it, and then if there is, you drop that one into the toilet, get more paper, and wipe again." But there really wasn't anything funny about it to him. He really wanted, and needed, to know. "That brown stuff?" he asked. "Yes." "Oh, okay." Next wipe, brown stuff. Next, clean paper, clean bum, happy boy. "I get it!" he exclaimed proudly. And he did. All of it. —t

----

4. See the good. Kids are doing lovely things for us and one another all the time. We parents often find ourselves commenting only in response to our child's negative behaviors, and as a result too much of our communication with our children is about what they're doing wrong. In doing this, we miss the opportunity to comment on what they're doing right. Our suggestion: make the effort to look for behaviors that exemplify thoughtfulness and responsibility and remark on them. "It was kind of you to help that girl collect her toys." "It was nice of you to let that boy have a turn with your shovel. The expression on his face showed how happy he was to have the chance to play with it." "Thanks for helping your sister put on her shoes. That was a big help to me, too." Focusing on the good things makes them feel appreciated and—no surprise here—reinforces the good stuff. And it feels much better as a parent, too.

5. Tell a story. Enhance learning and understanding by connecting an experience your child has with a real or fictitious story. Populate the narrative with characters she can relate to. Create any outcome you like. You can tell a story from "the other child's perspective," and the hurt feelings in your story can be those of a giraffe or monkey—amazingly—on the very same playground that you just returned home from. A little spider can be a character that worked so diligently and created something beautiful without anyone looking only to have the web torn apart by the wind. The once-scary monster can be called home and tucked into bed lovingly by his own Mama. Stories allow your child distance and perspective. They can provide vocabulary and a safe context in which to discuss something troubling or complex, exciting or amazing. If it is a lesson you want your child to learn, you can help them see the effect of their actions without directly blaming or shaming them. Sharing real stories from your own childhood can also show your understanding of their experience and allows your child to connect to you in a very meaningful way.

- -

This tactic has served me so many times! One that will always stick with me is the night we realized, at bedtime, that my daughter's favorite stuffie, Bessie the Horse, was left at preschool. Overnight. In a dark building. With no one there. A federal case, widespread panic, wailing grief. A quickly spun story, populated with characters from the fantasy world of her preschool, came to the rescue!

Mother Squirrel, who lived in the schoolyard tree, had snuck inside with her babies to see if Room Mouse had found any good snacking fodder left by the children or a lazy broom. They came across Bessie in Olivia's cubby, and immediately called all of the critters to a party in her honor … (with great commotion and mess, the toys came to life and prepared a feast and made mischief all through the classrooms—particularly with glitter and googly eyes—and had the time of their lives). Olivia fell asleep to this story, and the next morning couldn't wait to get to school to see if the teachers had done a good job cleaning up the mess. —t

- -

Toys That Aren't

1. Flashlight
2. Ace bandage
3. Rubber gloves
4. Rope
5. A lot of something

The ideas that follow are our favorite additions to the old stand-bys of large cardboard boxes, sheets, and pieces of fabric. Open-ended toys that don't have a predetermined way that they "should" be played with, or that don't come with a script from the latest blockbuster or TV show, require children to use their imaginations and come up with stories of their own.

---

1. Flashlight

… or headlamp! Shadows, outer space exploits, miner, explorer, theater spotlight, pretend camping adventures, spy games, flashlight tag.

2. Ace bandage

Vet hospital, emergency room, horse hooves … the velvet rope at a theater, a security line at the airport.

3. Rubber gloves

Scientist, explorer, gardener, construction worker. Inflated? An udder, a chicken comb, sea creature, alien.

4. Rope

A laundry line on the frontier, or key feature to any pulley system; a leash, a towline, a poisonous snake, a harness, a utility belt, a lasso (all with appropriate adult supervision, of course!).

5. A lot of something …

… like small, smooth rocks; buttons; beads; bottle caps. Whatever the item, the goal is to collect a lot of 'em. Rocks morph into birds' eggs, goat food, horse droppings in a mystery that must be solved. Buttons, beads, or bottle caps are currency, treasure, or lined up into designs.

Feeding the Family

1. Create traditions
2. Share real work
3. Take turns making a plan
4. Make it a date
5. Mark it with an X

1. Create traditions. Many families build traditions around the various holidays they celebrate. But we suggest creating and formalizing additional rituals, unique to your family, which can really add a sense of closeness—like the good old secret handshake from our imaginary childhood clubs. These practices get us to celebrate the little, everyday things. In our house, when someone is sick and staying home from school or work, we get out the special sick tray. Meals and snacks are brought to the patient on the special tray in bed—a bonus for having to miss school and lay low. To celebrate accomplishments, we break out the special glasses (small port glasses work well) and give the kids mocktails or "kids' wine" (i.e., grape juice). You can ask your children to propose events to celebrate about each other. Someone gave up diapers or a pacifier—a great cause for celebration!

Our family has created our own dinnertime ritual (a pseudo-grace if you will) in which we hold hands and say "Yay for our family" and then focus on each member of our family one at a time, saying, "Yay for Kate, yay for Will, yay for Zan, yay for Mommy, yay for Daddy," and conclude with "Yay for our family!" Often when grandparents or an aunt and uncle are visiting, one of our children proudly suggests, "Let's do 'Yay for our family.'" Sometimes the silliest and simplest things are the ones that stick, the ones that will be touchstones in family memories. —n

2. Share real work. Kids really feel valuable and connected when they share in the activities that support a household, whether it's cooking or cleaning, gardening or laundry. Most tasks have pieces that even the youngest children can take on with success. When you're not in a hurry or committed to doing something your own way (because there are those days, too), let your kids help change the batteries, mix up stuff in the kitchen, take lint off of the dryer screen, spackle a hole, sort laundry, set the table, dig in the garden, pull out weeds, match socks, or vacuum a room. Sharing work gives children a chance to learn things that are really useful and gain appreciation for the work that goes into a family.

I could not believe how excited my kids were to wash windows! They could barely wait their turns to squirt the window cleaner and polish the glass. I had to laugh about how long I had been dreading the chore and putting it off, yet they thought it was such a blast. —t

3. Take turns making a plan. It is all too easy for parents to be dictators when it comes to the slate of activities for shared family time. "Okay everyone, we're going to the park," or "Time to run errands." Amid busy family life, make it a point to occasionally carve out time for each child to decide what the family will do based on their own interests. For younger children, you can help them initially by asking for something they like and morphing it into a family activity. If the littlest member loves her stuffed animals, involve the older children in making an animal farm or hospital. Build an airport with blocks, or play school. Put on a puppet show, or make a parade. Kick a ball outside, or go to the playground. Hesitant? Start small (30 minutes) and insist that everyone get on board. These activities are not only good for the one who gets to choose but also for the ones who learn to participate in and contribute to someone else's idea. Taking turns making a plan highlights each individual's important contributions to a family unit and allows the rest of us to practice sharing, good team membership, and compromise.

4. Make it a date. Create opportunities for one-on-one time. Set aside time for just mother and son, father and daughter, or two sibs. Cultivating individual relationships within your family strengthens the parts that make the whole. Whether it is a special breakfast at a favorite diner, going for a walk, quiet reading or drawing together, an outing to bowl, a bike ride, leisurely shoe shopping or a trip to the library, the time to connect is what's important.

- -

While we try to have these dates regularly, they have been particularly key during times of transition. A number of months after our son was born we knew that Caroline, our middle child, had been making some difficult adjustments, certainly a few of them around sharing parents and her sister with a needy, nursing infant. We planned a "mama date" together—she wanted to go to a bookstore and sit in my lap while I read books to her, and then go to a restaurant and eat lunch. Though she was not even three, she still remembers what books we read and that she had pasta with butter, a roll, milk in a fancy glass, and ice cream for lunch that day. —t

- -

5. Mark it with an X. If your family calendar tends to fill up with back-to-back and overlap, make a point to set aside time. Go ahead, put a big "X" through a day on your calendar. No play dates, no grocery runs, no checking on work from home. Be open to anything; see what evolves and go with it. Whether it be a two-hour breakfast, a whole family basement clean-out, or a walk to explore the neighborhood, the only goal of this day is to be together. This is family time. And hey, no two X days will ever be the same, for any single family or between families.

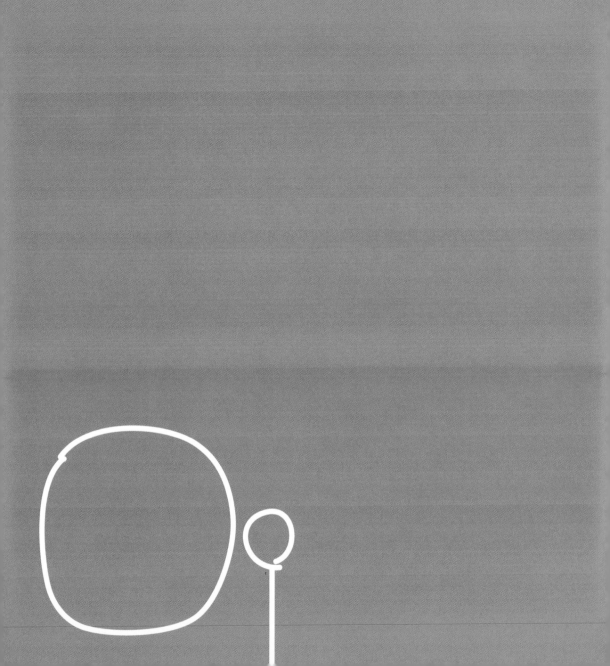

Mealtime Tricks

1. Go for a dip
2. Spice it up
3. Have breakfast for dinner
4. Put them to work!
5. Make it a game

1. Go for a dip. Sometimes changing the mode of eating can add a little excitement to the mealtime routine. Abandon the utensils and try dipping! Go beyond the fries and ketchup. Get cut veggies, breads, or meats and dip! Some of our favorites dips include hummus; ginger-miso dressing; soy and mayo; baba ganoush, yogurt and cucumber tatziki; olive oil, garlic, and grated Romano or Parmesan cheese; ranch dressing. Consider toothpicks or chopsticks for another twist.

2. Spice it up. Often the tendency is to assume children prefer simple and uncomplicated tastes. Don't be afraid to expose your kids to spices and spicy foods at a young age. Many young palates really welcome the more robust flavors. My daughter, who would only eat white food, suddenly took an interest when we started adding garlic and cayenne pepper to her meals. We discovered that she likes anything with curry or ginger. Take note when they say, "Mmm, that smells good!"

3. Have breakfast for dinner. Shake things up and make breakfast for dinner. It can be a fun little twist, with the added bonus of being an easy-to-make nutritious meal. Easy prep, yummy food: why save that for just the beginning of the day? French toast or pancakes with cottage cheese and fruit is a favorite, along with any kind of eggs and toast. It even smells like morning!

4. Put them to work! What kid doesn't take pride in something they make themselves? We've found it useful and fun to get buy-in to a meal by involving our kids. Whether it is assembling their own creations at the table or helping you prepare the meal, let them choose their own fillings for a burrito among avocado, tomato, beans, ground beef, sautéed onion, and cheese ... and let them pile it in. Each child's burrito can then be called the "[insert your child's name] special." Or let them mix, stir, and add ingredients as they help you assemble a dish. When age appropriate, tearing salad, picking the leaves off of basil or parsley, or chopping soft things such as tofu, hard-boiled eggs for egg salad, or cooked carrots can be fun for them and real help to you. And if they are interested in tasting along the way, all the better!

5. Make it a game. No, we don't advocate playing with food, but ... try these two games that are big hits in our house to introduce foods and make mealtimes fun. First: "taste-offs." Can your child taste the difference between a yellow, red, and orange pepper? How about broccoli three ways: raw, steamed, and with Parmesan?

You can have table-side chats about which they like and why. Or try the household favorite called "surprise bite." You can even use this catchy jingle as a preamble: "Open your mouth and close your eyes and you will get a big surprise." You then create a bite with a few different things from their plate. The contestant guesses which foods were in the bite or how many different foods were included. You can mix it up with questions about color categories, or what food groups items belong to.

Note: There is very little in the way of promise, reassurance, or catchy jingle that would get my kids to close their eyes for me to slip an unknown something into their mouths. This could be considered a game for the brave! —t

Stuck Indoors: Feeling Restless

1. Hunting: treasure or scavenger
2. Freeze dance
3. Rat house
4. Obstacle course
5. Beach ball or balloon games

1. Hunting: treasure or scavenger. Hide some kind of treasure and create a series of clues that lead from one to the next guiding your "treasure hunter" towards it. Some ideas: for pre-readers, draw a picture of a fork to lead them to the silverware drawer, a milk carton to the inside of the fridge, a pillow to their bed. Draw a bookshelf and point to a certain shelf. Make clues for early readers with simple words or phrases, and so on. "Scavenger hunters" collect things around the house from a list you make. Lists can be filled by random objects you choose (book, spoon, stuffed animal), or by descriptive categories (begins with "B," is round, soft, or red, or comes in a pair).

2. Freeze dance. This works best if you have a remote control for your music source. Play music in the widest open space in your home. Dance around with the kids, or get them to imitate you, or follow you ... then pause the music and hold a goofy pose. Start the music back up and keep it going.

3. Rat house (a.k.a. "pillow pile" or "fort"). Take the cushions off the couch, pile pillows and blankets into a big heap, and let kids burrow around in there. Or be more architecturally minded and build some kind of structure to get into. Definitely a big-scale mess, but a surprisingly simple clean-up compared to many art projects or toys with little pieces.

4. Obstacle course. Create a circuit, again in your widest open space, where kids have to climb over, crawl under, go around, jump three times, etc. Some ideas: toss a soft ball into a ring or bucket, jump two-footed over a series of blocks, make a tower out of a pile of blocks, crab walk backwards. Ask them to make up new parts to add to the course. Add a timing dimension to see if they can beat their previous time. Ask them to do it in reverse.

5. Beach ball or balloon games. Inside versions of volleyball work pretty well with balloons. For just one child, a balloon creates a great game of "keep it up," in which you try not to let the balloon touch the floor. And a beach ball allows for "catch" or an indoor soccer game. Our toddlers loved to play "foosball" (with parents swinging them) with a beach ball indoors.

Stuck Indoors: Feeling Mellow

1. Recorded books
2. Scrounge projects
3. Listen to music
4. Three-things & other stories
5. Shadow games

1. Recorded books. Toss some pillows on the floor, get comfy, and enjoy listening to a story—together, or let your kids have some downtime alone. Check out the selection at the library. A great recording can draw a listener into any story. Listening to recorded books is also our favorite long-car-ride strategy with our kids—find stories that are geared to their age level. No mess, no clean up.

2. Scrounge projects. Make something out of stuff found around the house. "Scrounge" in our house refers to all of that stuff that goes into the recycling bin (toilet paper tubes, cardboard, lids, plastic containers) as well as things like pieces of scrap paper, ribbon, buttons, popsicle sticks, and pipe cleaners. Scissors and masking tape work pretty well to join things together, while glue tends to be a little frustrating. Many a robot has been brought to life over a table full of scrounge!

3. Listen to music. Put on something you like, something relaxing, something featuring a certain instrument (piano, cello, guitar, etc.), or something that has a story to tell. Rediscover how listening as an activity is vastly different from putting on background music. Again, check the library for different genres. Lying on the floor somehow makes this more fun.

4. Three-things & other stories. Up for telling a tale of your own? Have your child come up with "three things" (e.g., cat, cake, lawnmower) and weave them into a silly story that features what they choose. Using your child's name makes it even better. Don't stress about your story not being interesting enough. "Once upon a time there was a cat named Joe, who secretly planned to bake a cake for his friend, Kate, who was having her third birthday party … just then a lawnmower ran into the cake … mowed, pieces flying everywhere … sad cat … small pieces of cake … mice and chipmunks and chickadees all come with their babies … celebrate … happy ending." (You get the idea.) If your child's up for it, give them three words and let their creative juices run. Or, collaborate on a "chain story" where each of you takes a turn saying a sentence or two about what happens next.

5. Shadow games. Take turns choosing objects that have to be guessed by the shadow image they make. We discovered this game while lying with our heads in one of those pop-up baby tents in our living room. There was a plastic lobster on the flat "roof" section of the tent, and the light in the room created a flat shadow against the "ceiling" we were looking up at. The lobster created a very cool shape, indeed. We were hooked. Now that we have moved beyond the baby tent, we play the shadow game with a sheet. Just be sure to secure it well and don't put anything too heavy on top. Try out some of these shapes: animals of all species (small plastic or stuffed), a CD, cutlery or kitchen gadgets, socks, a comb, small and familiar toys or teethers, toothbrush, a pinecone ...

Tips for Talking

1. Reference details
2. Listen
3. Be positive
4. Skip the rationale
5. Ask good questions

1. Reference details. If everything our children do is met with a generalized label of "the best" or "fabulous" from us, they'll eventually catch on that we're not very discriminating. When you comment on something your child has done, make a point to reference specific details. For example, "You really got the shape of that dog's ears in your drawing. You must have looked very carefully." "It must have taken a lot of practice to learn that song. I enjoyed hearing your class sing it." "I noticed how you lined up your shoes. You are taking good care of your things." When we call out these specifics, it demonstrates that we've taken the time to notice something they've worked hard at, whether it's a drawing or new table manners. When you do praise (which we all love to do!), leave the superlatives behind. Noticing specifics will ultimately be more meaningful to them than having everything they do labeled as "wonderful." We've also found when we make it a habit to refer to the details of the effort—rather than praising the outcome—our kids have been more likely to stay engaged in the tasks at hand.

2. Listen. By this we mean really listen ... like with full attention. When we show children that they matter and that we take them seriously, that we value their opinions and explanations—they know it. A few pointers we all know but sometimes forget: get down to their level rather than stand over them. Make eye contact. Be patient, and remember it takes children a little longer to express their thoughts verbally. And try not to finish their sentences or interrupt, even if you are doing it to show your interest and excitement. Again, be patient. Good conversations have a give-and-take that requires listening and responding to what has been heard. Modeling this allows kids to practice an important social skill.

Furthermore, when we really listen, we are more open to insights they might offer. What they tell us can be key to resolving perplexing issues, both simple and complex. A case in point: A parent we knew was confused by her child's reluctance to use the bathroom at preschool, since this was no problem at home. During the parent's lengthy conversation with the school director trying to ascertain the cause of this discrepancy in behavior, the child interrupted: "Mommy," she said, "But I can't reach the toilet paper here."

- -

My son had a very hard time separating at preschool. Mornings before school involved his protesting, "I don't want to go, I don't like school." I knew from his teachers he seemed quite happy during the day, and the morning struggles didn't seem to fit. One day he blurted out, "Just don't say goodbye!" Initially I thought he wanted me to stay at school again. But after some discussion, I realized that he was telling me exactly what he needed: it was the actual saying "goodbye" that was causing his anxiety. From then on I walked him to a teacher, did an about face, no words, no touches, walked to my car and drove away. This was very hard for me, but he happily went to school from then on. Finally, near the end of the year, he said, "You can take me in today and you can say good-bye," and I did. —n

- -

3. Be positive. It's a given that having young children often requires us to bark quick warnings to head off disaster: "Don't touch that" (very-fragile-glass-thing that's teetering on the edge of that shelf in this exceptionally expensive store!) or "Don't eat that!" (crusty-brown-thing you found on the side of the road). When there's less urgency, however, think about shifting to a positive tack. "Walk," rather than "don't run." "How about the trash?" rather than "Don't leave that on the ground." A gentle-but-firm positive suggestion feels better and produces a better outcome.

4. Skip the rationale. We often use a litany of reasons following simple requests made to our children: "It's time to go because you're tired, and it's late, and you have to get up early tomorrow, and you've had a lot of junk food, and it's really

noisy here, and … " Perhaps it makes us feel better to provide reasons for everything, thinking that they will hear our logic and do what we want willingly. But too often what follows the request doesn't add in a positive way. We start listing, nagging, or letting the "rationale" grow to include all of the little things, pulling in evidence to mount against the anticipated rebuttal. Ironically, by doing so we further charge the situation. When it's time to leave a party or playground, a simple "it's time for us to go" is what we should say, and what they need to hear. If what is being asked is straightforward and not up for debate, keep it short and sweet and skip the rationale.

5. Ask good questions. "How was it?" "Good." "Did you have fun?" "Yes." Sometimes that's the beginning of the conversation and often the end. Certainly there are times when we, too, aren't feeling chatty, but kids can often be encouraged into deeper and more meaningful conversations with the right parade of questions. Whether it's getting more details or helping them reflect on a particular experience, the right questions can help. If you want a play-by-play, drop anchor in a shared moment and let questions guide them through an account of their day: "What did you do after I left?" "Then what happened?" Sometimes specific questions work to get things started: "Who did you sit next to at circle time?" "Who was the attendance helper today?" Sometimes more vague works: "Tell me more about that picture … ." We don't advocate a daily inquisition, but if there's been a tough situation with a friend, something didn't go well, or when you simply want a deeper view into your child's world, unpack your questions and see what comes up! Some suggestions:

If something didn't go well

What did you try?

What did her expression say to you?

How could I have helped?

For artists and poets

What did it smell like (taste, feel, sound, look)?

What shapes or colors did you notice? How did they fit together?

Why do you think it made you feel that way?

For the litigator, engineer, or when inquiring minds want to know

How did it start? What happened next?

What happened right before then?

Would he tell the same story?

- -

I overheard this conversation at a playground. A girl came to her mother indignant at having been pushed by a boy. Trying to figure out the whole story, the mother asked, "What do you think that boy would be saying to his mom about what happened? "Oh," said the girl, completely guileless, "he'd say that I hit him in the face with a stick." —t

- -

Be an Enabler

1. Let them own it
2. Don't fix it
3. Leave space
4. Wait for them
5. See how smart

1. Let them own it. By this we mean, don't let parental praise become the motivating factor for what your child does. When kids are driven to do things in order to be recognized, the value of their actions—and thus the importance of the effort—becomes misplaced. Most children know when they've done something well and feel genuine pride in their accomplishment. Yes, kids want our approval, and they do need to know that we see their efforts. However, our admiration shouldn't be the endgame—their own sense of fulfillment should be the goal.

2. Don't fix it. Resist the urge to "fix" something not done to your sense of perfection when your child has completed a task and he seems pleased with the result. Don't straighten out the blanket on the bed he made. If he put away groceries, leave the can of beans on the shelf he chose. Don't refold the laundry that he proudly helped you with. Resist the urge to correct the backwards Zs and Ss when he is first learning to write. No matter what you say, it sends him the message that what he did wasn't good enough.

3. Leave space. Children benefit from space in their days that requires them to come up with their own fun. Creating their own fun is a valuable skill that can take time to learn and develop. These days there are so many options for child-focused activities. The caring parent in us wants to expose them to things early; the anxious parent worries about being left behind when it seems the whole neighborhood is heading off to lessons and games. Will they be able to keep up with their peers if we don't start soccer at four? If we don't do tee-ball will they miss their shot at the high school team? What about music, isn't early exposure important? A friend mentioned taking her child to a Spanish class, should I be doing that?

It's easy to feel like your child will be missing out on something if you don't sign them up for every possible activity. But when we think of self-motivation (e.g., creating their own fun) as a skill we want for our kids as much as athletic proficiency or musical competence, we are more likely to carve out time and "leave space" for it to develop. So, when it comes time to sign up or try out, be thoughtful and deliberate about how you fill their days.

4. Wait for them. Introduce new things when your child is ready. There's nothing more frustrating for a child than a toy or task intended for an older child. No, it really won't help them develop faster. They won't get smarter sooner, or learn something earlier. A puzzle with too many pieces will just frustrate your clever three-year-old. This idea applies as well when your child is starting something new. As an example: If a child is learning to separate from a parent at preschool, stick to a plan with modest goals. If your son was meant to stay just an hour without you and he's doing fine at the end of that hour, don't give into the temptation to stretch the time. Go pick him up while he's happy. Wait for him to be settled enough that he craves a little more. Building on small successes gives kids a sense of accomplishment and stability, and there is great value (and pride) in them being the ones who come up with the desire to stay longer at school or try the higher slide at the park.

5. See how smart. There is a lot of information out there about various types of "intelligence," but many of us still tend to measure our children and ourselves in the narrow categories of verbal and mathematical ability. Parents of even the youngest children claim bragging rights if their child speaks at a young age, can recognize letters or starts counting before others in the playgroup. There are a lot of ways to be "smart," and many areas in which to excel. Kudos to the parent who sees and supports their child in all the other places kids might find a foothold: music (the kid's got rhythm!), nature (has an affinity for growing things? collecting things? animals?), spatial relationships (great at building and puzzles?), or sports. Hooray for the parent who recognizes that their child is exceedingly kind, compassionate, self-aware or friendly with others, and celebrates that.

Out and About Adventures

1. Self checkout
2. Pet store
3. Public transportation
4. Take me out to a ballgame
5. Car wash

1. Self checkout. Why "play store" at home when you can actually get some shopping done? Lots of stores now have self-checkout aisles. For kids it's a blast. At a fairly young age they can scan, use a touch screen to choose a payment method, and collect change and the receipt. They can work up to keying in the code for bananas or choosing the type of container for produce. If you can, go at midday, when stores aren't busy. Not an activity for a major stock-up, but for a modest number of items, it's a real winner.

2. Pet store. While a zoo or aquarium can be a special excursion, a pet store has always been a favorite destination for our animal lovers. Swing by during an afternoon of errands or for a low-key activity on a rainy day. Beware of the request for pets that may follow. Be clear at the outset that this is a looking or visiting trip.

3. Public transportation. If you live near public transportation, and usually drive to get from here to there, an outing simply for the ride can be a big treat. Kids ride free, there's no car seat: what's not to love? The bus, the train, the subway—each is an adventure waiting to happen. Add an ice cream cone or a picnic and you've got yourself a terrific low-budget outing.

- -

My son's favorite activity at age three was riding the bus. We would get on at the stop near the end of our street, ride to the end of the line, get off, turn around and board the next bus to come home. He loved the bus sign at the stop (and looking for others along the route), the sturdy place to put the coins in for the fare, the driver's seat with the accordion base that bounced smoothly over bumps. I loved that we were simply going somewhere and being out among people. I loved that I didn't have to concentrate on driving, that he could sit in my lap and look out the window, that we could point out landmarks together and just talk. —t

- -

4. Take me out to a ball game. Find a local little league or high school soccer game. Take a blanket and some snacks. If your child is interested, explain the game. Many fields offer a nearby playground when interest wanes. Little league offers the chance to sit in the bleachers and be a part of a cheering crowd without the price tag or commitment to a major league game.

5. Car wash. There are two versions of this one, depending on the age of your child. One option is the ride-through, fully automated car wash. This is a quick burst of entertainment: first the squirting water from all angles, then the spinning sudsy brushes, the long stringy brushes slapping to and fro on the hood, and the rinse followed by the super high-powered dryer that blows the windshield wipers in the air. Or try the coin-fed, do-it-yourself methods.

- -

My kids love to help me take out the car mats, position the nozzle, and wait with anticipation as I drop the coins in to start the super vacuum. They then look around trying to help me locate every piece of sand or food remnant before our quarters run out. "There's some here, Mommy!" For more excitement, you can move onto the main event with the high-powered hose and sudsing brush. —n

- -

- -

Note: When I was little, there was nothing more terrifying to me than the drive-through car wash. Our entire family in our station wagon would get swallowed whole into the belly of the beast, and I would hold my breath until we were safely out the other side. Something to keep in mind—this may not be for everyone! —t

- -

Smoothing the Bumps

1. Surrender 15 minutes
2. Tend to the victim first
3. Keep in mind: this, too, shall pass
4. "Puppetshow it!"
5. Say "yes" when you can

1. Surrender 15 minutes. Balancing children's demands and a parent's desire to get things done is one of the hallmark struggles of having young children. Some days it feels like you can't even use the toilet in peace, let alone take a shower or return a phone call. When tensions mount and you are ready to lock yourself in the garage and scream "When do I get MY time?" try the unexpected and counterintuitive. Give in. Drop everything and surrender 15 minutes and do whatever your child wants. Sit and read, build with blocks, let them sit on your lap and type letters on the keyboard. Lavish them with love and attention. Too often these moments when children seem particularly needy or clingy are when they feel us, their parents, pulling away into our own worlds. Show them that we're still here for them in the most over-the-top way and then they may wander off content. (And then, if you want, you can check your email!)

One of my most successful strategies for a clingy child, which always took far fewer than 15 minutes, was what came to be known as the "Never-Go-Away Cuddle." I'd sit with them on the couch and hold them like when they were babies. I'd tell them how we don't really need to eat or go outside ever again, that everything I needed was right here in my lap and lo! we could even sleep here, so comfy this was … They would laugh through this, and little by little try to plan their escape, which, of course, I would theatrically thwart. The crazier the "things we could do without" were that I rattled off as we sat together, the funnier they thought it was. As the children got older, they would actually ask for these "Never-Go-Away Cuddles." It has always been five minutes well spent. —t

2. Tend to the victim first. As parents we all witness countless scuffles among young playmates and siblings. When a child is injured, most of us would agree on the importance of caring for the injured party first and sorting out "who started it" later. In addition, there are two situations where tending to the victim first (and ignoring the perpetrator) can be a dramatic game-changer: when a child (particularly one's own) is being aggressive to get attention, and when kids are fighting over

a toy. When a child becomes the aggressor to gain adult attention, tending to the victim first really alters the dynamic by taking the power out of the behavior that was meant to get a reaction. When a child sees the adult tending to the victim and not focusing on them, she will be encouraged to move onto other (hopefully more positive) methods of getting noticed. And then there is the very common situation of two children fighting over a toy. One tactic we've used with success is to animate the toy (i.e., the toy becomes the "victim") and give it your attention in a very dramatic way. By doing so you can offer children a new perspective, and teach a lesson about respect and behavior that may just find a deeper understanding than if you had corrected or reprimanded them directly.

_ _

One day at preschool I witnessed two girls fighting over a doll—an all-out tug of war. One was pulling her hair and the other pulling her legs. Rather than addressing the children and admonishing them to stop and share, a teacher gasped loudly (so now many children turned their heads) and ran over saying, "Oh, poor Dolly! Oh, my! You come with me, are you okay? You must need a little rest!" She took the doll and walked to the other side of the room, cradling her and saying soothing things. Boy, did that diffuse the tiff! —n

_ _

3. Keep in mind: this, too, shall pass. All things have a beginning and an end. Sleepless nights, hitting, potty training, whining, teething. Pooping in the neighbor's bushes. Childhood. When our kids are in the middle of particularly challenging phase or engaging in infuriating behavior, it is easy to lose sight of the fact that these, too, shall pass. Consider if there may be any contributing factors and how you might address them: new developmental stages always rock the boat — learning to walk or talk; eating solids; new work schedule for a parent; new family structures—and then let it go. Give yourself a break and trust that most things are a phase and will end soon.

4. "Puppetshow it!" That's the verb phrase my son made up to ask me to animate objects to make whatever we were doing a little more palatable or fun. When you have a tired kid or want to add some fun to the more routine parts of the day, we say "puppetshow it!" Almost anything can have a puppet alter-ego. Make the washcloth "eat" the breakfast mess off your child's face while it comments on the morning's offerings in a silly voice: "Mmmm eggs! And ummm, JAM! And what is this way over here? Did you eat something with your ear?!" Have a favorite doll administer the medicine your child may be reluctant to take. A jacket left on the floor can ask to be hung up next to "his" friends. My kids will often more happily do things when asked by my "crane" (that's just my hand) than when it's me (and my "regular mouth") doing the talking!

5. Say "yes" when you can. By this we mean look for—and be open to—more chances to say "yes." This powerhouse tactic can do three things: smooth the bumps, affirm your child, and help you emphasize the boundaries that are most meaningful.

It can be dismaying how frequently, in the face of parenting exhaustion and stress, our knee-jerk response to children's desires is "no." When tensions rise, we try to call upon the little mantra, "Can I say yes here?" It often finesses the way forward. "May I have another cookie?" "Can I drink out of one of those cups?" These straightforward requests can sometimes be indulged to get over a hump or reward a patient child. Most of us are nagged by the fear that this kind of indulgence might lead to bad habits or spoiled kids. Remind yourself that there don't need to be hard and fast rules: on some days it might be okay to have the extra cookie, and on others not. Likewise, for some families some options are a possibility, and for others not. "Yes, you may have another cookie" (because you were really cooperative while we were running errands, and I appreciate it), or maybe it's "not now" because dinner is almost ready. "Yes, you may drink out of that cup" (but only water). "Yes, but—" can sometimes work wonders. Hooray! You are still in charge!

There are also opportunities to say "yes" to requests that are often brushed aside because we are in a rush. These are chances to affirm your child—to show them that you take them seriously. While it might seem silly to us to "take the ramp instead of the stairs," if your kid noticed the option and asked, then it's likely important to him. Be open to those seemingly silly requests—they are great opportunities to let your child feel appreciated with very little effort on your part. Riding the escalator at the mall one more time will add three minutes to your day but will show your son that what he cares about is important to you. Rather than thinking of it as an indulgence, consider it an affirmation.

"Saying 'yes' when you can" also means loosening up your parenting style. We've found these small shifts to "yes" actually serve to set apart the truly important boundaries (about respect for others, health, and safety) that we establish for our families rather than creating a situation that leans toward pint-sized anarchy and indulgence. Like the rest of us, children respond to rules when there are fewer of them. When the frequent little "nos" drop away, the bigger "nos" become clearer and better heard. Children are then more apt to pay attention to the boundaries that really matter. But when those principles aren't in question, we say give that extra cookie, ride the escalator again, and, more generally, "Say yes when you can."

just the lists...

Thoughts for Newbies

1. Find your people
2. Let go
3. Find your own way
4. Embrace a new rhythm
5. Back off

Gifts to Yourself

1. Care for your friendships
2. Share a passion
3. Give yourself a head start
4. Learn something new
5. Get out!

Teaching and Learning

1. Share the thinking
2. Let discovery happen
3. Break it down
4. See the good
5. Tell a story

Toys That Aren't

1. Flashlight
2. Ace bandage
3. Rubber gloves
4. Rope
5. A lot of something

Feeding the Family

1. Create traditions
2. Share real work
3. Take turns making a plan
4. Make it a date
5. Mark it with an X

Mealtime Tricks

1. Go for a dip
2. Spice it up
3. Have breakfast for dinner
4. Put them to work!
5. Make it a game

Stuck Indoors: Feeling Restless

1. Hunting: treasure or scavenger
2. Freeze dance
3. Rat house
4. Obstacle course
5. Beach ball or balloon games

Stuck Indoors: Feeling Mellow

1. Recorded books
2. Scrounge projects
3. Listen to Music
4. Three-thing & other stories
5. Shadow games

Tips for Talking

1. Reference details
2. Listen
3. Be positive
4. Skip the rationale
5. Ask good questions

Be an Enabler

1. Let them own it
2. Don't fix it
3. Leave space
4. Wait for them
5. See how smart

Out and About Adventures

1. Self checkout
2. Pet store
3. Public transportation
4. Take me out to a ballgame
5. Car wash

Smoothing the Bumps

1. Surrender 15 minutes
2. Tend to the victim first
3. Keep in mind: this, too, shall pass
4. "Puppetshow it!"
5. Say "yes" when you can

about the authors

Tara and Nina met in the throes of parenting when their kids attended the same cooperative preschool in Watertown, Mass. Their contrasting personalities and life experiences led to rich conversations on parenting topics. These conversations—and a mutual love of lists—inspired this book. Tara and Nina each brought to this project what they bring to their friendship: Tara—creativity, calm, and a few more years of the parenting road behind her; Nina—enough energy for everyone, and an uncanny ability to ask good questions and get stuff done. In her rare spare time, Nina works hard to stay in touch with friends and family, hunts for bargains, and thinks about lunch while she's having breakfast and dinner while she's having lunch. Tara is happiest when she's heading out for a run, whipping up hearty vegetarian creations, or scouting out local haunts for great live music. They both "say yes when they can" in the greater Boston area, where each lives with her husband and three children.